You Can't Eat Toes For Breakfast

written by Rickey Teems II
illustrated by Laurie Barrows

Text © 2012 Rickey TeemsII

NoGuile Books
PO Box 30675
Los Angeles CA 90030

www.noguilebooks.com

Illustrations & Design ©2012 Laurie Barrows   133

www.LaurieBarrows.com

ISBN 978-0-9832226-3-7

Printed in the United States of America

Published in the United States of America

Dedicated to Munchie,
You are loved from your toes to your nose!

George, breakfast!
Get your food while it's hot.
It gives strength and energy.
Superheroes need that a lot!

I looked all around,
not a bad guy in sight.
So I flew to the table,
ready for my first bite.

Wash your hands and say grace,
you know how it goes.
Oh, what kind of jelly
do you want on your toes?

Did Mom go insane?
Was she losing her brain?
Eggs, bacon, and cereal, everyone knows.
But who ever heard of eating breakfast with toes?

Toes help us balance.
I use mine to reach high.
I'm not going to eat them.
Nope, I won't even try.

Next she might ask me to eat my feet.
Then how will I stand or run in the street?
Then I'd have to give up my favorite shoes.
I'm not eating feet. Mom must be confused.

And don't even think of putting legs on my plate.
I use them to jump, walk and to skate.
Legs make me taller, and I want to grow.
Don't feed me legs, Mom. Thank you, but no.

Is she looking at my arms?
Uh-uh, those are mine!
I need them to throw, reach and to climb.
I'm grateful for arms. I use them every day.
We can't eat my arms, Mom. Sorry, no way!

My hands aren't an option, so don't even ask.
I use them to write, hold, wave and to grasp.
They're for giving high fives and sign language too.
No hands for breakfast, Mom. No thank you!

For all I know, next she'll want ears,
and leave me with absolutely no way to hear.
How would I tell if things are far or near?
No music? No sound? No listening clear?
No way to hear? Not even a peep?
Thanks for the offer, but my ears I will keep!

And it would be no surprise, if next she says eyes.
Then how would I read, or see clouds in the skies?
No teacher's chalkboard or nature outside?
I'll skip eyes for breakfast, not scrambled or fried!

And serving my mouth, I hope she doesn't think!
I use teeth to chew and my lips help to drink.
I like my tongue, plus, hello, I need to speak!
Can't eat my mouth, not now or next week!

And my nose is off limits. I still need to smell.
Sweet, sour or spicy, how could I tell?
I couldn't wake and smell the roses, if we eat my nose.
What a horrible idea. That's worse than eating toes!

Mom, I'm sorry, but I'm not gonna do it!
This is my body, I won't bite it or chew it.
Breakfast is important, but hey, so am I.
We can't eat my toes, Mom, so don't even try!

Oh George, you're so silly.
I love you the most!
You're not breakfast or lunch or a dinner roast!
I didn't mean toes, I meant bread as in toast!
I need you complete, from head to feet.
You're sweet for hugs 'n kisses, but not to eat!

Just a big mistake! I'm so relieved!
No need to change Mom's mind with my mind changing machines.
Breakfast is soooo important. Good nutrition is a must!
Just eat toast and not toes, take it from us!!